Stars & Planets

Stars & Planets

CONSULTING EDITOR

David H. Levy
Senior Instructional Specialist, University of Arizona

WELDON OWEN

Contents

• OUR UNIVERSE •

• EXPLORING THE UNIVERSE •

Early Astronomers

Long ago, people thought that the Earth was flat and the sky was the home of great gods. They told myths and legends to explain night and day, the changing of the seasons, and the sudden appearance of strange, "long-haired stars" (comets). The ancient Chinese, Babylonians and Egyptians were the first to record the movements of the heavenly bodies. The Greeks proved that the Earth was round and tried to work out the order of the universe by charting the stars and planets they saw. Claudius Ptolemy, a Greek astronomer, believed that the Earth was at the centre of the universe, and the Moon, the Sun, planets and stars all revolved around it. Ptolemy's view was accepted for nearly 1,500 years, but in 1543 a Polish astronomer and priest Nicolaus Copernicus suggested that the Earth and the other planets orbited the Sun. This view caused much anger and debate because people believed that the Earth was the most important planet. With the first telescopes, which were built in the 1600s, people were able to expand their view of the universe.

PTOLEMY'S PICTURE
Claudius Ptolemy pieced together a picture of the universe, but he mistakenly put Earth at the centre of it. As astronomers developed special tools, such as telescopes, they realised that many early theories about the universe were incorrect.

AN EARLY ASTRONOMER
Nicolaus Copernicus published his astronomical ideas in 1543. People were still arguing about his theories years after his death. Galileo and later astronomers helped to prove that many of his ideas were true.

LOOKING TO THE STARS
Skywatching is an ancient pastime. Our ancestors gazed at the Sun, the Moon, the bright planets, comets and meteors. The study of the sky, astronomy, has developed from people's desire to understand how these heavenly bodies relate to each other and to the Earth.

DID YOU KNOW?

More than 4,000 years ago, these giant stone slabs were placed carefully in a circle at Stonehenge in England. It seems that people may have watched and recorded the times and positions of the rising Sun and Moon from this ancient site.

SKYWATCHING
Tycho Brahe was a great sixteenth-century astronomer. In 1572, he saw a star as bright as Venus in the constellation of Cassiopeia. This strange new star was a supernova—the brightest one in 500 years.

CALENDAR OF EVENTS

The ancient Babylonians and Chinese developed the earliest calendars, based on the rising and setting of stars throughout the year. The ancient Egyptians noticed that the bright star Sirius reappeared in the eastern sky (after several months of not being visible) just before sunrise for a few days each year. As the River Nile began to flood shortly after this sighting, they fixed their calendars around the time of this event. The fifteenth-century calendar on the left is English, while the sixteenth-century calendar on the right is Danish.

EASTERN ZODIAC SIGNS
These are some of the standard astrological signs for Chinese and other eastern astrologers. They use them to define the areas where the planets travel.

Tiger

Dog

Mouse

Horse

Cow

Rooster

SIGNS FROM ABOVE
Ancient observers thought they saw patterns or figures in the night sky. From left to right, the picture above shows the constellations of Leo, Cancer, Gemini and Taurus.

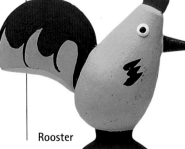

• INTRODUCTION •

Astronomy and Astrology

Early skywatchers studied the stars, kept records of the movements of the planets and compiled calendars. The night sky seemed a magical place with strange, unexplained forces and they interpreted what they saw by creating myths and legends about the gods who lived in the sky. They imagined they could see shapes in the patterns of the stars (constellations), and they named them after mythological characters, such as lions and hunters. Twelve of these constellations lie close to the yearly path of the Sun in the sky (called the ecliptic). We call this band of sky the zodiac. Astrologers believe that the heavenly bodies exert an influence on people's affairs, personalities and futures. They predict events for the different signs of the zodiac based on their observations of happenings in the sky. Astronomy, however, is the scientific study of the universe. Astronomers have learnt much about the universe, but they have found no evidence that it directly affects the lives of people on Earth.

8

WESTERN ZODIAC SIGNS
The word "zodiac" means "circle of the animals" in Greek. Most of the 12 constellations of the western zodiac, shown here, are represented by animals.

CONSULTING THE STARS

Astrologers were important people in ancient society. People believed that the position of the Sun and the planets in the sky influenced their lives and that some days would be better than others for certain activities. This army general is consulting an astrologer before drawing up his battle plans. Today, some people still see an astrologer before making decisions.

Discover more in Enjoy the Sky

The Universe

The Earth and the other planets, the stars, the galaxies, the space around them and the energy that comes from them are all part of what we call the universe. Most astronomers believe that between 8 and 16 billion years ago, all matter and energy, even space itself, were concentrated in a single point. There was a tremendous explosion—the Big Bang—and within a few minutes the basic materials of the universe, such as hydrogen and helium, came to be. These gases collected together into large bodies called galaxies. Today, the universe still seems to be expanding. Huge families, or superclusters, of galaxies are racing away from all the other clusters at incredible speeds. If the Big Bang has given them enough energy, the galaxy superclusters may keep on racing away from each other until the last star has died. But if their gravity is strong enough to slow them down, everything in the universe will eventually cascade in on itself in an event we call the Big Crunch. Then, perhaps another cycle will begin.

The Big Bang | 100,000 years later | 1 billion years later | 8 billion years later | 13 billion years later (now)

BIG BANG
The Big Bang took place long ago, but most of its work was accomplished in a very short time. Hydrogen was created quickly, and the galaxies began to form soon after. As stars within these galaxies exploded, the heavier elements, such as carbon (the basis of life), were formed.

A SMALL PART OF A LARGE SCHEME
We live on the Earth, just one planet in the solar system. Our solar system is part of the Milky Way, just one galaxy in a cluster of galaxies. These clusters gather into superclusters of galaxies, all of which are expanding outward.

NIGHT SKY

The ceiling of stars we can see on a clear night is a tiny part of the universe, which is immense in both time and space.

BIG CRUNCH

The expansion of the universe will be reversed if gravity is strong enough to pull everything together again.

Close

Closer

Closer still

The Big Crunch

BACK TO THE PAST

In 1965, scientists Arno Penzias and Robert Wilson were testing a radio antenna when they detected strange energy emissions. They searched for the source of these emissions and soon made a staggering discovery: the universe had a very weak level of radiation. The existence of radiation confirmed the theory of some astronomers that the Big Bang had left a cool afterglow in space. In 1978, Penzias and Wilson won the Nobel Prize in Physics for discovering this important fact about the beginning of the universe.

Discover more in Galaxies

The planets closest to the Sun move around their orbits faster than those farther away. The Earth takes a year to complete its orbit. The planets also spin around as they orbit the Sun. The Earth spins once every 24 hours, which we call a day. Here we show the different sizes of the planets, as well as the time they take to orbit the Sun (given as a year) and to spin on their axis (given as a day).

Mercury
Year: 88 Earth days
Day: 59 Earth days

Venus
Year: 225 Earth days
Day: 243 Earth days

Earth
Year: 365.25 days
Day: 24 hours

Mars
Year: 1.9 Earth years
Day: 24.6 hours

Jupiter
Year: 11.9 Earth years
Day: 9.8 hours

DID YOU KNOW?

Pluto takes 248 years to circle the Sun and for most of that time it is the farthest planet from the Sun. But Pluto has a very oval-shaped orbit, and for 20 years of its total orbit, Pluto is actually closer to the Sun than its neighbour Neptune.

• OUR NEIGHBOURHOOD •

The Solar System

Humans live on a small planet in a tiny part of a vast universe. This part of the universe is called the solar system, and it is dominated by a single brilliant star–the Sun. The solar system is the Earth's neighbourhood and the planets Mercury, Venus, Mars, Jupiter, Saturn, Uranus, Neptune and Pluto are the Earth's neighbours. They all have the same stars in the sky and orbit the same Sun. Scientists believe the solar system began about 5 billion years ago, perhaps when a nearby star exploded and caused a large cloud of dust and gas to collapse in on itself. The hot, central part of the cloud became the Sun, while some smaller pieces formed around it and became the planets. Other fragments became comets and asteroids (minor planets), which also orbit the Sun. The early solar system was a turbulent mix of hot gas and rocky debris. Comets and asteroids bombarded the planets and their moons, scarring them with craters that can still be seen today.

PLANET PATHS
The Sun is massive and has a strong gravity that pulls the planets towards it. The planets also have their own energy of motion and without the pull of the Sun, which bends the planets' paths into orbits around it, they would fly off into space.

Saturn
Year: 29.5 Earth years
Day: 10.2 hours

Uranus
Year: 84 Earth years
Day: 17.9 hours

Neptune
Year: 165 Earth years
Day: 19.2 hours

Pluto
Year: 248 Earth years
Day: 6.4 Earth days

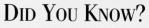

The Sun

The Sun is the centre of the solar system. This enormous star gives us all the light and heat we need to grow food and keep warm. It was worshipped as the mightiest of the gods by the ancient Egyptians. The Sun, however, is not the largest star in the galaxy. It seems very big and bright because it is only 150 million km (93 million miles) away from Earth. Light from the Sun takes eight minutes to reach us; light from Sirius, the next brightest star, takes eight years! The Sun is made up of gases, mostly hydrogen, and is powered by a natural process called nuclear fusion—when atoms of hydrogen fuse or join together to make helium. Nuclear fusion takes place in the centre, or core, of the Sun, where temperatures are around 15 million°C (27 million°F). The Sun has shone in the sky for nearly 5 billion years and scientists believe it has enough hydrogen in its core to "burn" for another 5 billion years. Then it will expand to become a red giant before shrinking to become a feeble white star.

DID YOU KNOW?
The corona is as hot as the centre of the Sun. However, the gases inside the corona are very thin because the gas particles are very far apart. This means that if you put your hand into this searing heat, you would not feel a thing.

CLOUD ACTIVITY
Clouds of gas called prominences can erupt from the Sun's surface. They are best seen during a total eclipse of the Sun—when the Moon cuts off the bright light of the photosphere.

INSIDE THE SUN
Energy is produced in the core of the Sun. It is transferred to the surface through the body of the star—the zone of radiation and convection. We can see the Sun's photosphere through the thin chromosphere and the outer atmosphere—the corona.

THE SURFACE OF THE SUN
This picture shows the boiling surface of the Sun. Cool, dark patches called sunspots lie beneath the bright spots seen here.

ENERGY BURST
Solar flares are huge eruptions that occur near sunspots. They release a massive amount of energy into space.

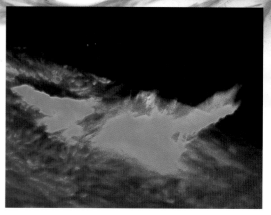

Sunspots

Core

Convective zone

Radiative zone

Photosphere

Chromosphere

RIBBONS OF LIGHT

Solar flares send charged particles from areas around sunspots into space. When they hit the Earth's charged upper atmosphere near the magnetic poles, they cause colourful dancing ribbons of light, called auroras, or Northern or Southern lights. Auroras appear more often when there is heavy sunspot activity.

Mercury and Venus

For at least half a billion years after the solar system was
born, the planets were battered by debris. The surface of
Mercury is pockmarked with craters from this time, just as
the surface of Earth must once have been. Unlike Earth, however,
Mercury has no air or water to wear these craters away. As it is
the closest planet to the Sun, Mercury speeds swiftly through
the sky, like the winged Roman god after which it is named.
But because Mercury is so close to the Sun, it is very hard
to see in the night sky. Venus, however, is the brightest
"star" in the morning or evening sky. Shrouded in a layer of
clouds, the surface of Venus is more than four times as hot as
boiling water. Even at night, the temperatures remain high.
Like the Earth, Venus is heated by the Sun, but the
thick canopy of clouds and carbon dioxide
makes it impossible for this heat
to escape. Venus is a scorching
and extreme example of the
greenhouse effect.

A MELTING POT

The surface of Venus is a furious
mingling of elements. As a volcano
belches lava, a rain of hot sulfuric
acid falls from the sky onto the
hot ground. Lightning strikes
punctuate the chaos.

MERCURY, THE FOSSIL PLANET

Steep cliffs and craters scar the surface of Mercury. The day on Mercury is searingly hot because the planet is so close to the Sun, but the night is unbearably cold. As Mercury has no real atmosphere, impact craters that were formed nearly 4 billion years ago still dominate its ancient surface. In 1977, the *Mariner 10* spacecraft visited Mercury and took some revealing pictures of the planet, such as the one shown here. These photos gave us a bleak picture of the early history of the solar system. Comets and asteroids regularly hit Mercury and all the planets during a time we call the "age of heavy bombardment".

DID YOU KNOW?

Venus is the Roman goddess of love, and most of the features on the planet Venus are named after real or imaginary women. Two of its continents take the names of the goddesses Ishtar and Aphrodite, and a crater is named after the famous jazz singer Billie Holiday.

A RARE EVENT
If you look very closely at this time-lapse photograph, you will be able to see a small dot, which is Venus passing behind the Moon. This rare event is called an occultation and it takes place when the Moon passes in front of a planet.

BRIGHT LIGHT
As its thick clouds reflect light back into space, Venus is by far the brightest planet in the sky. However, it is visible only before dawn or after dusk for a few months each year.

Discover more in The Solar System

17

The Earth

We live on a small planet—the only place in the solar system where life seems to flourish. Seen from an Apollo spacecraft orbiting the Moon, the Earth is a colourful planet of green spaces, deserts, deep oceans and fields of ice. Life on Earth is possible because our planet is just the right distance from the Sun for water to exist as a liquid. If the Earth was a few million kilometres either closer to or farther from the Sun, it might be a boiling cauldron such as Venus, or a frozen wasteland such as Mars or the moons of Jupiter. Life is also sustained by the Earth's atmosphere—a thin layer of gas that surrounds the planet. Of all the planets in our solar system, this atmosphere is unique because it contains so much oxygen. The Earth orbits the Sun, and spins like a top once a day. This rotation and the Earth's atmosphere keep temperatures from reaching extremes, such as those on the nearby Moon.

Crust
Mantle
Inner core
Outer core

INSIDE THE EARTH
The solid iron inner core of the Earth is surrounded by a liquid outer core, and a soft rock mantle. The rock structures we actually see are part of the crust, which ranges in thickness from 5–70 km (3–43 miles).

N: Spring
N: Summer
N: Wint
N: Autumn
S

THE FOUR SEASONS
The Earth's seasons are caused by the way the Earth tilts as it orbits the Sun. Through the year, the Southern and the Northern (N) hemispheres have opposite seasons: while the Northern Hemisphere has winter the Southern Hemisphere has summer.

THE MIDNIGHT SUN
At the equator, summer days are the same length as winter days. As you go farther north or south, the difference in length between winter and summer days becomes greater and greater. If you go far enough north or south, you will reach a place (such as Norway shown below) where on some summer days the Sun never sets.

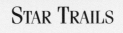

STAR TRAILS

The Sun moves across the sky as the Earth rotates. This picture shows that the stars also appear to move to the west, but it is really because the Earth is rotating towards the east. To take a picture such as this, leave your camera well mounted and its lens open for about half an hour. As the Earth moves east, the stars will appear to draw lines on the film.

VIEWING THE MOON

At any time, half of the sphere of the Moon is lit by the Sun. We might see just a little of the lit side (at crescent phase), most of it (in gibbous, or more than half, phase) or all of it (at full phase). How much we see depends on where the Moon is in orbit around the Earth.

HIGH AND LOW TIDES

Some places on Earth, such as the Fijian coast shown here, have extreme tidal ranges. The low tides expose much of the sea floor, while the high tides seem to sweep away the land.

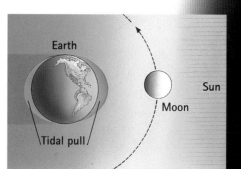

GRAVITATIONAL PULL

Tides are caused by the pull of the Moon's gravity, and to a lesser extent the Sun's gravity, on the Earth's oceans.

• OUR NEIGHBOURHOOD •

The Earth's Moon

People have been entranced by the Moon for centuries. The astronomer Galileo first looked through a telescope at this mysterious ball of rock in 1609. He saw its strangely uneven surface; its mountains and craters; and its dark, lava-filled basins (called "seas"), caused by collisions that rocked the Moon during the chaotic beginnings of the solar system. From the Earth, these dark markings seem to form a pattern, which people sometimes call a rabbit, a cat or even the "Man in the Moon". Astronaut Neil Armstrong became the first man on the Moon in 1969. The world watched in awe as he stepped on this airless, waterless satellite of the Earth. As the Moon moves around its endless orbit of the Earth, it seems to change shape in our sky, depending on how much of it is lit by the Sun. But we always see the same face of the Moon because it spins on its axis in the same time it takes to orbit the Earth.

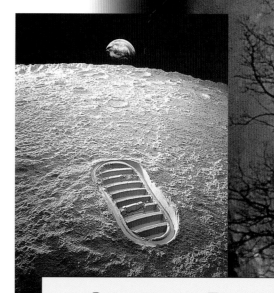

STRANGE BUT TRUE

When Neil Armstrong took "one small step for a man, one giant leap for mankind," the footprint he left was a permanent one. As there is no air on the Moon, Armstrong's footprint should last for many millions of years. Eventually, tiny hits from small meteoroids will cause the footprint to fade

How the Moon came to be is a subject of great debate. The best of the current theories says that a tremendous collision, early in the Earth's history, produced a cloud of rocky debris that orbited the Earth. The debris formed clumps that heated as they collected together. The result was a new body that cooled down to become the Moon.

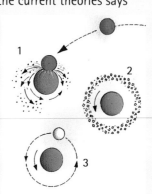

Mars

The Romans called the orange-red planet in the night sky Mars, after the god of war. Its surface is covered by rusty-red rock and dotted with huge canyons and volcanoes, polar icecaps and mountains. Phobos and Deimos, tiny moons scarred by craters, orbit the planet. Since the astronomer Schiaparelli first studied Mars in the late nineteenth century, people have wanted to believe that there was life on this planet. It is only half the size of Earth, but the planets are similar in some ways: the day on Mars is half an hour longer than ours, and it has changes in weather like our seasons. In the 1970s, space probes visited Mars but their findings showed that the red, rocky planet is like a chillingly cold desert. Water probably lies frozen beneath the hostile ground. The atmosphere on Mars is too thin to breathe, and violent dust storms sometimes howl across its surface.

THE LARGEST OF THEM ALL
Olympus Mons is the biggest volcano in the solar system. It is as large as the American state of Arizona! Olympus Mons rises so slowly that you could climb it without being aware that you were getting higher.

INTO THE FUTURE
A spacemobile such as this may one day be used to carry scientists across the surface of Mars to collect specimens from canyons and ancient river beds.

MARS ROVER
This vehicle has been built especially for exploring the surface of Mars. Its large wheels will help it travel across the rough terrain.

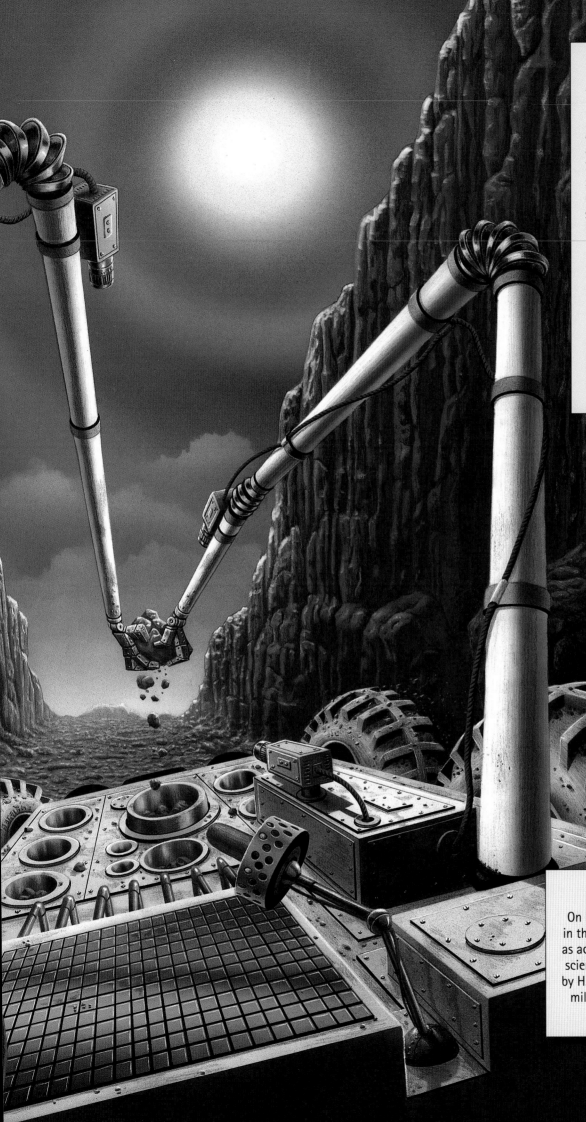

A FAMILY OF MOONS
Jupiter is surrounded by a large family of moons. Galileo saw Io, Europa, Ganymede and Callisto, the biggest and brightest of all Jupiter's moons, through a telescope in 1610.

COLLISIONS IN THE UNIVERSE
In July 1992, Comet Shoemaker-Levy 9 passed so close to Jupiter that it split into 21 pieces. Two years later, the comet fragments collided with Jupiter. Every large telescope on Earth and in space was poised to see the dramatic collision and the huge, spectacular fireballs that rose about 3,000 km (1,900 miles) above Jupiter's clouds.

• OUR NEIGHBOURHOOD •

Jupiter

Named after the king of the Roman gods, Jupiter is the largest planet in the solar system. It is 300 times heavier than the Earth and more than twice as heavy as all the other planets added together! The enormous gravity causes very high temperatures and pressure deep inside Jupiter. This stormy planet is cloaked by noxious gases such as hydrogen, ammonia and methane and topped by bitterly cold, swirling cloud zones, which change in appearance as the planet spins quickly on its axis. A day on Jupiter is less than 10 hours long–the shortest day in the solar system. This speedy rotation causes great winds and wild storms. Like most of the planets, Jupiter has moons. We know of at least 16 moons, but there may be smaller ones still to be found. In 1979, the *Voyager 1* space probe discovered that Jupiter was encircled by a narrow, faint ring made up of rocky or icy fragments.

THE MOONS OF JUPITER

Jupiter's four largest moons are very different from each other. Io, the closest of the four to Jupiter, has many volcanic vents that spew clouds of sulfur into the sky. *Voyager 1* recorded five erupting volcanoes when it visited Io in 1979. The smooth, icy surface of the next moon, Europa, is patterned with cracks that may once have been filled with water. The icy surfaces of Ganymede and Callisto, the largest moons, are marked by craters, the remains of ancient impacts.

Io   Europa

AS STORMY AS EVER

Astronomers first saw Jupiter's Great Red Spot 300 years ago. This swirling whirlpool of gases is a huge storm cloud that seems to rage constantly on this turbulent planet.

Saturn

The bright rings of Saturn are a dazzling highlight of the night sky. Ever since Dutch scientist Christiaan Huygens saw them through a telescope more than 300 years ago, astronomers have turned their sights to Saturn. From the Earth, it seems that Saturn is surrounded by three rings, but the 1981 Voyager space probe discovered that there are thousands of narrow ringlets made up of millions of icy particles. These ringlets stretch for thousands of kilometres into space in a paper-thin disc. The rings were formed long ago, perhaps when a moon or an asteroid came too close to Saturn and was torn apart by the strong gravity of the planet, which is the second largest in the solar system. Like Jupiter, Uranus and Neptune, Saturn is made up mainly of hydrogen and helium. It spins very quickly on its axis and is circled by bands of clouds.

Cassini's division
This has far fewer ringlets.

A LASTING IMPACT
One of Saturn's moons, Mimas, has a huge crater called Herschel. It was caused by a violent collision with a comet or an asteroid long ago, which nearly tore the little moon apart.

A ring
This is very bright where the ringlets are spaced closely together.

B ring
The colour of this seems to be more solid.

STUDYING SATURN

Saturn has a smooth, yellowish tinge, which is caused by a layer of haze that surrounds the planet. Unlike Jupiter, which it resembles slightly in colour, it does not seem to have any longlasting light or dark spots.

C ring
From Earth, this is seen as a faint ring.

Encke gap
This is a large gap within the A ring.

F ring
Seems to be knotted or plaited.

SATURN'S MOONS

Saturn has more moons than any other planet. Eighteen have been discovered so far, but there are probably smaller moons that we have not seen yet.

FAR FROM THE SUN

Orange-coloured Titan is Saturn's biggest moon. It is the only moon in the solar system with an atmosphere, which is made up mostly of nitrogen. As on Venus, this thick atmosphere hangs over Titan like a veil. Because it is so far away from the Sun, Titan is very cold and the methane on the planet is a liquid not a gas.

27

Uranus

Uranus is the Greek god of the sky. The planet was first noticed in 1781 by Englishman William Herschel, who saw a small round object with a greenish tinge through his home-made telescope. The discovery of Uranus caused great excitement. Astronomers had previously believed that Saturn lay at the edge of the solar system. As Uranus lies twice as far from the Sun as Saturn, the known size of the solar system suddenly doubled! Uranus is nearly four times the size of the Earth, and it orbits the Sun every 84 years. Like Jupiter and Saturn, it is made up mainly of hydrogen and helium. Most of the planets in the solar system are tilted a little (the Earth is tilted at an angle of 23°, and this causes the different seasons), but Uranus is tilted completely on its side. This means that each pole has constant sunlight for 42 years. When the *Voyager 2* space probe passed Uranus in 1986, it photographed the dense clouds that cover the planet, its narrow rings and its beautiful moons.

THE MOON MIRANDA
Miranda, the smallest and most unusual of the five main moons of Uranus, looms into view in front of the planet. This photograph was taken by the *Voyager 2* space probe as it flew past Uranus in 1986.

CLOSE-UP
Miranda has a unique surface. Some astronomers believe that it may have broken apart after a collision, but then re-formed. When the pieces of the moon came back together again, its surface was buckled with deep grooves.

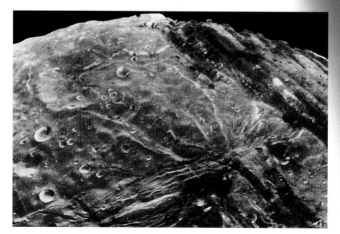

BEFORE
In the early days of the solar system, a large body may have crashed into Uranus.

AFTER
This collision tilted Uranus so that it rolls through the sky on its side.

DID YOU KNOW?
The rings of Uranus were discovered by astronomers in 1977. As Uranus passed in front of a star, they saw that the star's light flickered. They realised that rings around the planet were blocking the light of the star as they passed across it.

THE ROYAL ASTRONOMER

When William Herschel first observed Uranus, he thought he had discovered a comet or a star. His find proved to be much greater. King George III of England was so delighted with the discovery, he made Herschel his private astronomer. The king also gave Herschel the funds he needed to build larger telescopes, such as this.

Discover more in The Solar System

29

Neptune

Neptune is the smallest of the four gas planets and more than 3 billion km (2 billion miles) away from the Sun. Astronomers see a faint star when they view Neptune through a small telescope. This deep-blue planet is a bleak and windy place, with poisonous clouds made of methane ice crystals swirling around it. The planet's rocky core is about the size of the Earth, and is surrounded by a frozen layer of water and ammonia. Like the other gas planets, Neptune's atmosphere consists mainly of hydrogen. Neptune was discovered in 1846, but until *Voyager 2* sent pictures of it back to Earth in 1989, we understood very little about it. Now we know that Neptune has many faint rings and eight moons. The largest moon, Triton, is covered by ice and has mysterious features such as dark streaks. These could be caused by volcanoes erupting nitrogen, which becomes a liquid in Triton's intensely cold climate.

A BRIEF SPOTTING
Voyager 2 photographed this spinning storm cloud called the Great Dark Spot. Five years later, however, photographs from the Hubble Space Telescope showed that the spot had disappeared.

RULER OF THE SEVEN SEAS
The Romans believed that Neptune was the powerful god of the sea. His son Triton, who was half man and half fish, ruled the stormy waves with his father.

SURFACE ERUPTIONS
Triton, the Earth, Venus and Jupiter's moon Io are the only places in the solar system where there seems to be volcanic activity. But Triton's volcanoes are cold and erupt liquid nitrogen, not hot lava.

PICTURING NEPTUNE
The American space probe *Voyager 2*, shown here, was launched in 1977. Twelve years later, it reached Neptune on the distant edge of the solar system. Radio messages from the probe travelled to Earth at the speed of light.

THE DISCOVERY OF NEPTUNE

As astronomers in the nineteenth century plotted the course of the stars and planets in the solar system, they noticed that Uranus did not seem to follow its predicted orbit. Was the gravity from an undiscovered planet beyond Uranus affecting its orbit? Englishman John Couch Adams and Frenchman Urbain Le Verrier both calculated exactly where a mystery planet might lie. The German astronomer Johann Galle used their careful research, and in 1846 he became the first person to see the new planet through his telescope.

Far left: Urbain Le Verrier
Left: John Couch Adams

31

Pluto

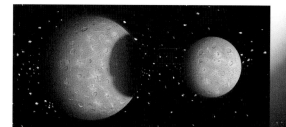

THE VIEW FROM SPACE
Pluto and Charon are very
close together. They
loom largely in
each other's
night sky.

Pluto lies in the far reaches of the solar system and is named after the Greek god of the dark underworld. This rocky planet is the smallest in the solar system and, usually, the farthest from the Sun. Pluto, however, has a strangely elongated orbit. It spends 20 years of the 248 years it takes to orbit the Sun inside the orbit of Neptune. Then it moves away and heads deeper into space. For most of Pluto's long year, the materials that make up its surface are frozen. But when Pluto moves closer to the Sun, some of these materials turn from solids into gases, and the planet has an atmosphere. Pluto was not discovered until 1930, and it has not yet been reached by a space probe. Although we know that it has a moon, called Charon, which takes about six days to circle Pluto, there is still much to learn about this distant speck in the night sky.

DID YOU KNOW?

Walt Disney, the famous American film-maker, created the droopy-eared cartoon character Pluto just a few months after the planet Pluto was found and named.

Neptune

Pluto

LOOPING THE LOOP

This diagram shows the oval-shaped orbit of Pluto around the Sun. Twice during its 248-year orbit, Pluto's path brings it closer than Neptune to the Sun.

THE VIEW FROM PLUTO

The shadow of the moon Charon falls on the icy surface of Pluto. Charon is half the size of Pluto, and Pluto is smaller than the Earth's moon.

THE SEARCH FOR THE MYSTERY PLANET

Astronomer Clyde Tombaugh (right) discovered Pluto in 1930. He had followed Percival Lowell's theories that a planet lay beyond Neptune, which could explain the irregular orbits of Neptune and Uranus. But astronomers soon realised that the discovery of Pluto did not explain this at all! Pluto was far too small to have such an effect on the planets' orbits. Some astronomers think that there is another, more massive planet farther away from Pluto. The search continues.

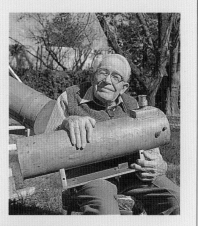

Comets

Comets are icy balls that sweep through the solar system. Long ago people thought these "long-haired stars", which appeared mysteriously and dramatically in the sky, were a sign that evil events were about to happen. Edmund Halley dispelled this idea in the eighteenth century by proving that comets, like all matter in the solar system, have set orbits around the Sun. Some comets pass near the Sun every few years. Others have long orbits and pass close to the Sun only once. As a comet gets closer to the Sun, its nucleus (centre) begins to warm up and gives off a cloud of dust and gas called a coma. Astronomers can see the coma through a telescope because it reflects the fiery light of the Sun and becomes much larger than the Earth. As the comet journeys towards the Sun, the solar wind blows a stream of dust and gas away from the comet and the Sun. This forms the comet's tail, a spectacular streak of gas and dust that can trail for millions of kilometres into space.

STRANGE BUT TRUE
People in the past believed that comets brought disasters. In the fifteenth century, astrologers for the Archduke of Milan told him he had nothing to fear, except a comet. Unfortunately, a comet appeared in 1402. The archduke was seized with panic when he saw it, had some kind of attack, and died.

Gas tail
This is straight, narrow and usually fainter than the dust tail.

Coma
This envelope of gas surrounds the nucleus of the comet.

Nucleus
This is a mixture of ice and dust. It gives off a cloud of dust and gas when it is heated.

CLOSE-UP OF A COMET
The nucleus is the dirty snowball at the heart of a comet. It is so small that it cannot be seen from Earth by the naked eye. But we can see the huge coma, and the gas and dust tail (or sometimes tails) that stream behind the comet.

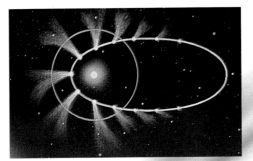

COMET'S TAIL
As a comet orbits the Sun, its tail grows and fades, but always points away from the Sun.

Dust tail
This is usually curved and is made up of gases pushed away from the Sun by the solar wind.

RETURN OF THE COMET

Halley's Comet is probably the most famous of all comets. Edmund Halley (top) was the first person to calculate that the appearance of three separate comets through the years was in fact the return of one comet every 76 years. The comet was named after him when he successfully predicted its return in 1758. In early times, Halley's Comet terrified those who saw it. In 1910, we had an opportunity to view the comet at close range as the Earth passed through the comet's tail. In 1986, spacecraft from different nations went out to meet Halley's Comet (bottom). The comet is now beyond the orbit of Uranus, east of the constellation of Orion. In 2062, Halley's Comet will once again brighten the sky.

COMET LEVY
Comets are often named after the people who first saw them. In 1990, Comet Levy lit the sky all night long.

Asteroids and Meteoroids

The solar system has many different members, the smallest of which are asteroids and meteoroids. Asteroids are small rocky bodies that never came together in the early days of the solar system to form larger planets. Most asteroids lie in the enormous space between the orbits of Mars and Jupiter, an area called the asteroid belt. Ceres, the largest of these asteroids and the first to be discovered, is almost 800 km (500 miles) wide. Most asteroids, however, are much smaller. Meteoroids are dust particles that travel along the orbital paths of comets. When a meteoroid encounters the Earth's upper atmosphere at high speed, it usually burns up and forms a bright meteor. Some people call this brief streak of light a "shooting star". Larger meteors that pierce the Earth's atmosphere and crash to the ground, making craters where they land, are called meteorites.

ASTEROID ORBITS

Not all asteroids orbit in the main belt between Mars and Jupiter (the larger planet in this picture). Two groups of asteroids called Trojans share Jupiter's orbit. Other asteroids cross the orbit of the Earth.

FLYING OBJECTS IN SPACE

On its June 1983 voyage, the space shuttle *Challenger* was hit by a tiny particle, possibly a meteoroid or a speck of paint left by a spacecraft on a previous mission. The shuttle and the small particle were travelling so fast that the impact left a small crater in the shuttle's window (below). Even the tiniest object moving at high speed is dangerous in space.

DID YOU KNOW?

In 1992, an asteroid called Toutatis passed close to Earth and astronomer Steve Ostro was able to bounce radar signals off it. From the reflection on the radar, he was able to work out that Toutatis actually looked like two asteroids close together.

LOOK OUT BELOW!

These children are standing next to one of the largest meteorites in the world. Long ago, the Inuit (Eskimos) of Cape York in Greenland worshipped this object from the sky.

MAKING ITS MARK

Astronomers calculate that large asteroids collide with the Earth every hundred thousand years or so. This crater at Gosse Bluff in the Northern Territory of Australia is the result of such a collision.

Discover more in The Solar System

Impacts in the Solar System

About 3.9 billion years ago, in the early days of the solar system, bright comets and asteroids orbited the Sun. These huge bodies bombarded the planets and caused enormous damage, such as the craters we can see on the Moon, Mercury and Mars, and which were once visible on Earth. Many scientists believe that the impact of a comet or an asteroid on Earth may have played some part in the extinction of the dinosaurs 65 million years ago. Impacts in the solar system caused great devastation, but it seems that they may have also made it possible for life to begin on Earth. When comets from the cool outer reaches of the solar system struck the Earth, they released carbon, hydrogen, oxygen and nitrogen into the Earth's atmosphere (these had been lost early in the Earth's history). These organic materials are essential to life forms. Life itself is based on carbon, while hydrogen and oxygen make up water (H_2O), without which plants and animals could not survive.

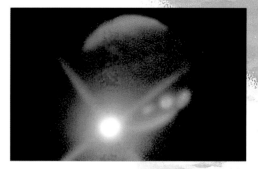

IMPACTING STILL
Major impacts still happen today, but not usually on Earth. In July 1994, Comet Shoemaker–Levy 9 collided with Jupiter and caused several brilliant explosions.

DID YOU KNOW?

Impacts on the Earth have been worn away by erosion and the movement of the Earth's crust. The Moon, however, still shows the scars of impacts that happened several billion years ago.

IMPACTS ON EARTH
In this imagined scene, a *Tyrannosaurus* is interrupted from its meal by shattering sounds and lights as a comet hits the Earth. A major earthquake soon follows, and temperatures become as high as boiling water. A thick cloud of debris settles over the whole world, bringing months of darkness, cold and sulfuric acid rain. Many species of life eventually die in such conditions.

EARLY IMPACTS
Impacts in the early solar system were very common. When a huge body such as this collided with the Earth, it may have formed the Earth's Moon.

When the Moon is near its full phase, you can see a number of dark areas. Most of these areas are huge impact basins—the lava-filled remains of ancient collisions. If you look at the Moon with a pair of binoculars or a small telescope, you will also see many craters on its surface—the results of asteroid or comet crashes.

STAGES OF A LUNAR ECLIPSE

These photographs show the progress of a lunar eclipse, from the first bite of the Earth's shadow on the Moon's surface to the total phase and beyond.

Eclipses

The Sun sends its light far into space. As light falls on the Earth and the Moon, both cast a shadow. An eclipse of the Moon (a lunar eclipse) occurs when the shadow of the Earth darkens the Moon. The Moon sometimes becomes coppery red or even brownish as the Earth's shadow marches across its surface. An eclipse of the Sun (a solar eclipse) occurs when the Moon passes in front of the Sun and blocks the light to places along a narrow strip of the Earth's surface. A strange darkness falls on the land and temperatures drop. The Moon is 400 times smaller than the Sun, but it can hide the light of such an enormous star because the Sun is so far away from the Moon. When we look at the Sun and the Moon in the sky, they appear to be almost the same size. Solar eclipses occur in cycles. One eclipse will be very similar to another that happened more than 18 years earlier, but they will not be at the same place.

CLOAKING THE SUN

Eclipses can be either partial, if only part of the Sun or Moon is covered; or total, if the whole is hidden from view. This time-lapse photograph shows the progress of a total eclipse of the Sun. The Moon takes just over an hour to cover the Sun completely. It hides the light from the Sun's surface and allows us to see the Sun's faint, ghostly corona.

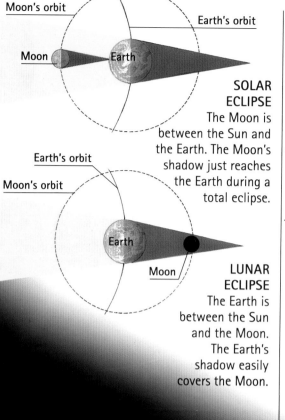

SOLAR ECLIPSE
The Moon is between the Sun and the Earth. The Moon's shadow just reaches the Earth during a total eclipse.

LUNAR ECLIPSE
The Earth is between the Sun and the Moon. The Earth's shadow easily covers the Moon.

VIEWING A SOLAR ECLIPSE

Eclipses are unforgettable sights that we would all like to see, but the Sun is very dangerous to look at without proper protection for your eyes. Permanent blindness can result from the shortest look through binoculars or telescopes. The eyepiece filters that are often supplied with small telescopes are not safe either. The girl in this picture is safely viewing an eclipse without a telescope. With the Sun behind her, she holds a piece of paper with a hole through it. The light passes through the hole and projects an image of the eclipse onto another piece of paper in front of her.

Discover more in The Sun

The Life Cycle of a Star

Picture a huge dark cloud (a nebula) in space. When a nearby star explodes, a shock wave travels through the cloud. The cloud begins to shrink and divide into even smaller swirling clouds. The centre, called the protostar, gets hotter and hotter until it ignites and a new star is born. All the stars in the sky were born from clouds of gas and dust. The hottest stars are blue-white in colour and burn their hydrogen fuel very quickly. The Sun, a small yellow star, burns hydrogen more steadily. Proxima Centauri, the closest star to the Sun, burns its gas very slowly and is a cool, red star. The speed at which the stars burn hydrogen determines how long they will live. Blue giants have a short life, and explode dramatically. The Sun will continue to burn for another 5 billion years. Then it will expand into a large red giant and finally shrink to a white dwarf. Proxima Centauri, however, will remain unchanged for tens of billions of years.

THE ORION NEBULA
Orion is one of the best known group of stars (constellation) in the sky. Some 1,600 light years away and 25 light years wide, the Great Nebula in Orion is a stellar nursery, a place where new stars are being born out of interstellar gas.

Nebula
This is a huge cloud of hydrogen, helium and microscopic dust.

White dwarf
After the planetary nebula disappears, all that remains is a small, hot, faint star.

Planetary nebula
Later in its life, a star slowly blows off its outer layers to form a planetary nebula that eventually disappears.

THE CYCLE OF LIFE
The main diagram shows the different stages in the life of a star, such as the Sun. This kind of star lasts for many billions of years. As it uses up its hydrogen, it begins to swell and will become, briefly, as large as the orbit of the Earth. Then it will shrink to become a white dwarf, slowly cooling for many billions of years.

Protostar
The centre of the nebula gets hotter as it shrinks, finally creating a new star.

Life of a star
Massive stars live for perhaps several hundred million years. Smaller stars last for many billions of years.

A BLACK HOLE

After a very heavy star uses up its hydrogen and explodes as a supernova, its core becomes smaller and smaller until finally it is smaller than the head of a pin. The star, however, still has gravity. This is so strong that even light from a few kilometres around the star cannot escape. This is called a black hole.

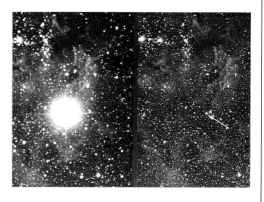

A SUPERNOVA
For a few days, a supernova (above left) can outshine an entire galaxy of hundreds of billions of stars. Then it becomes a tiny dot, as shown by the arrow.

THE HORSEHEAD NEBULA
A nebula is a bright or dark cloud made up of gas or dust, or sometimes both. The Horsehead Nebula is very dark and can only be seen against a background of stars or a bright nebula.

Red giant
Late in its life, a star grows to form a red giant with an enormous surface area.

Discover more in Asteroids and Meteoroids

43

Strange Stars

Stars are giant balls of hot gas. Their range of size, colour, temperature and brightness varies enormously. They can be members of a pair, triplet or a huge cluster of hundreds or thousands of stars. The colour of a star indicates how hot it is: cool stars are red, hot stars are bluish. Many of the stars studied by astronomers are in pairs and orbit each other. These "binary stars" often differ in brightness and colour: a dim white dwarf, for example, might orbit a red giant. Stars that make up a binary pair are usually a great distance from each other, but some are so close they almost touch. These stars are called contact binaries and as they are so close, they have to orbit each other very rapidly. The smaller star is very dense and its gravity constantly sucks hydrogen gas away from the larger star. The big star becomes distorted and turns into a distinctive teardrop shape.

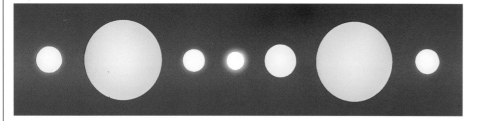

A CHANGE OF SIZE
Some stars grow bigger and smaller, as shown above. The most famous and important of these are called Cepheid variables. Their colour, temperature and brightness change with their size.

QUICK FLASHES
A small, extremely dense neutron star is often all that remains of a star after it has become a supernova. It rotates in a second or less and if we see the quick flashes we call it a pulsar.

A MEETING OF MATTERS

In this contact binary system, the large star looks much more impressive and powerful. But the small, dense star has the real power. It has a stronger gravitational pull than the big star and is able to drag matter away and distort the shape of the large star.

EXPLODING STARS

What happens to all the hydrogen that the small star takes from the large star in a binary star system? The small star has no use for it and the hydrogen collects in a disc. When enough hydrogen has built up, over months, decades or possibly centuries, it blows up in a huge nuclear explosion. The star brightens 100 times or more for a few days. Once the explosion has died away, the process begins again.

Discover more in The Life Cycle of a Star

Galaxies

Galaxies are enormous families of stars, which lie scattered across the never-ending space of the universe. Each galaxy contains many millions of stars—a mixture of giant and dwarf stars, old and young stars, and clusters of stars. Some galaxies are spiral in shape, while others are elliptical (like a flattened circle). Those that do not seem to have much of a shape at all are called irregular galaxies. There are countless numbers of galaxies, and they are grouped together in clusters. Our solar system, for example, is part of the Milky Way Galaxy. This belongs to a collection of galaxies called the Local Group, which contains about 25 galaxies, such as the Large and Small Magellanic Clouds. The Andromeda Galaxy, the largest member of our cluster, is so huge we can see it in a very dark sky without a telescope. It lies more than 2 million light years away from Earth. Light reaching us now from the Andromeda Galaxy began its journey across space long ago when the earliest humans lived on Earth.

NEIGHBOURING GALAXY
The spiral Andromeda Galaxy is the nearest major galaxy to the Milky Way. It contains hundreds of billions of stars and its spiral arms are mottled with bright and dark nebulae.

A GROUPING OF GALAXIES
The universe has a natural order. Galaxies occur in clusters that gather into larger superclusters.

SPIRAL
The arms of a normal spiral galaxy are filled with stars and gas clouds.

BARRED SPIRAL
A barred spiral galaxy has a bar of stars across its centre. The spiral arms begin at the ends of the bar.

ELLIPTICAL GALAXY
Giant elliptical galaxies are massive. This galaxy has 5 trillion stars.

IRREGULAR GALAXY
Irregular galaxies have random shapes and they are smaller than the Milky Way.

A LIGHT FROM THE EDGE OF THE UNIVERSE

Quasars are extraordinarily powerful beacons, scattered deep in the universe. The word "quasar" stands for "quasi-stellar" (resembling a star), but quasars have far more energy than stars. A quasar called 3C-273 is several billion light years away from Earth, yet it is bright enough to be seen with a large amateur telescope. Such brilliance suggests huge size, but quasars are probably less than one light year across. Astronomers believe that a quasar is a black hole at the center of a distant galaxy, which consumes all the matter around it. The whirling matter being sucked into the hole creates an amazing source of energy and powerful "jets" of material (right), which are projected out of the galaxy's glowing core.

Discover more in The Universe

The Milky Way

On a clear night, the sky is speckled with thousands of stars. In fact, these are just a few of the 200 billion stars belonging to our galaxy, the Milky Way. From Earth, the thickest part of the Milky Way looks like a patchy band of white light stretching into space. But the Milky Way is actually shaped like a spiral, and is about 100,000 light years across. It has at least two major arms, made up of dusty nebulae and brilliant blue-white stars. Older yellow and red stars form the nucleus of the galaxy. As Earth lies way out on one of the arms of the galaxy, 30,000 light years from the centre, it is very difficult for us to imagine what the galaxy looks like from the outside. Clouds of dust and gas also block much of our view of the middle of the galaxy. Astronomers, however, have recently determined that a huge object, possibly a black hole, lies in the centre of the Milky Way.

A VIEW FROM THE UNIVERSE
The Milky Way would look like a mighty spiral of stars, gas clouds and dust if viewed from one of the distant globular clusters.

48

STUDYING THE MILKY WAY

Astronomer Bart Bok (below) and his scientist wife Priscilla Fairfield devoted their lives to unravelling the mysteries of the Milky Way. By careful observation, they mapped out the spiral arms of the galaxy. They also studied the great clouds that illuminate the sky in the constellations of Orion and Carina, and tried to piece together how new stars are born from these clouds.

OUTSIDE LOOKING IN

If you could look at the Milky Way from the outside, you would see a central bulge surrounded by a thin disc that contains the spiral arms.

Discover more in Galaxies

49

Into Space

In 1957, Russia launched the first artificial satellite, *Sputnik 1*, into orbit. The Space Age had begun. Four years later, Russian Yuri Gagarin became the first person in space, and President Kennedy declared that the United States would put a man on the Moon by the end of the decade. In 1969, the *Apollo 11* spacecraft, attached to the biggest rocket ever built, pierced the Earth's atmosphere and headed towards the Moon. Astronaut Neil Armstrong's first words and steps on the scarred surface of the Moon soon became history. In the last 30 years, we have explored and discovered much about space, the stars and the planets. Spacecraft have flown past all the planets and their moons, except Pluto on the edge of the solar system; there have been several expeditions to the Moon; and space probes have landed on both Mars and Venus. Space shuttles are sent regularly into space as workhorses. Their crews sometimes repair the many satellites orbiting the Earth, such as communication satellites, which send telephone and television signals all around the world.

PROBING SPACE
The Japanese space probe *Tenma* looks at objects in space, such as black holes and supernovas, which have much energy.

LIVING IN SPACE
This is an imagined space station of the future. It is much bigger than the Soviet Mir space station, which was launched in 1986. People are aboard Mir most of the time, and the longest stay by one person so far has been a year.

LAUNCHING INTO SPACE

Space shuttles are very special spacecraft. They are designed to be used many times, taking heavy objects, such as space probes, around the Earth; and carrying crews for scientific research into space. They have three parts: an orbiter, an external tank, and two solid rocket boosters. The first space shuttle in 1981 carried two astronauts. Today, they can take a crew of up to eight people.

ON THE MOON

Even the simplest tasks require great planning and patience in the low gravity of the Moon. This astronaut is collecting a rock sample, which will be examined back on Earth.

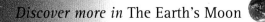

Discover more in The Earth's Moon

Imagined Worlds

A CITY ON MARS
In an imagined world on Mars, a spaceship prepares to land on the red surface of the planet. A space base, where people live and carry out research, has been built in the shelter of a deep valley.

Is there life on other planets? Astronomers and science-fiction writers have considered this question for years. Aliens, mutant monsters and other life forms, both menacing and friendly, have starred in many books, films and series, such as *Star Wars* and *Star Trek*. People all over the world regularly report sightings of Unidentified Flying Objects (UFOs) and encounters with strange beings from space. Is this fact or fiction? Many astronomers believe that life-forming conditions do exist elsewhere in the Milky Way. For many years, people looked to our solar system and thought that Mars was the other planet most likely to support life. Technology has now made it possible to study Mars in detail and this idea today seems unlikely. Much of space, however, remains unknown territory. Science-fiction writers imagine worlds and events beyond our own. In 1865, writer Jules Verne predicted that we would reach the Moon. Some of our imagined worlds may also come true.

ANYONE OUT THERE?

In New South Wales, Australia, the Parkes radio telescope has been listening to the heavens for more than 30 years. But in 1995, as part of Project Phoenix (a worldwide search for life in outer space), the telescope examined areas around some nearby stars for regular signals that could come from intelligent life. The normal levels of radiation in the universe produce a random noisy hiss. If a radio telescope picks up a more orderly signal, such as that from a radio transmission, this could be evidence that life exists elsewhere.

WORLDS AWAY
The covers of these science-fiction magazines from the 1920s show strange forms of life on Neptune (right) and Venus (far right).

A CITY ON NEPTUNE
The complete story of this city of the Reptile Men is told on page 144

STRANGE BUT TRUE

The distances in space are astronomical. In order to move from one star system to another, the makers of *Star Trek* developed the idea of travelling at what they called warp speed, which is many times faster than the speed of light. Such speed would be essential to make travel between the stars possible within a human lifetime.

Facts and Figures

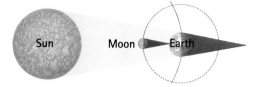

SOLAR ECLIPSES

Solar eclipses can be partial (when only a part of the Sun is blocked from the Earth's view), total (when the Sun is totally blocked from the Earth's view) or annular (when the Sun's light is still visible from around the edge of the Moon).

DATE	TYPE OF ECLIPSE	AREA FROM WHICH ECLIPSE CAN BEST BE VIEWED
17 April 1996	partial	New Zealand, Antarctica, South Pacific
12 October 1996	partial	Greenland, Iceland, Europe, North Africa
8–9 March 1997	total	Russia, eastern Asia, Arctic, northwest North America, Japan
1–2 September 1997	partial	Antarctica, South Pacific, New Zealand, Australia
26 February 1998	total	Pacific, Central America, Atlantic, West Indies
21–22 August 1998	annular	Malaysia, Indonesia, Philippines
16 February 1999	annular	Australia
11 August 1999	total	Atlantic, United Kingdom, Europe, India
5 February 2000	partial	Antarctica
1 July 2000	partial	Southern Chile
31 July 2000	partial	Northwest Canada, Siberia, Alaska
21 June 2001	total	Angola, Mozambique, Zambia, Madagascar
14 December 2001	annular	Costa Rica, Nicaragua

LUNAR ECLIPSES

Lunar eclipses can be either partial (when the Moon is only partially covered by the Earth's shadow) or total (when the Moon is totally covered by the Earth's shadow).

DATE	TYPE OF ECLIPSE	AREA FROM WHICH ECLIPSE CAN BEST BE VIEWED
3–4 April 1996	total	Africa, South America, Europe
27 September 1996	total	Nth America, Central America, Sth America, Europe, Africa
24 March 1997	partial	North America, Alaska, Hawaii
16 September 1997	total	Asia, Africa, Europe, Australasia
28 July 1999	partial	North America
21 January 2000	total	North and South America
1 July 2000	partial	Southern Chile
16 July 2000	total	Pacific Ocean, Australia, eastern Asia
9 January 2001	total	Asia, Africa, Europe
5 July 2001	partial	Australia, eastern Asia

SELECTED MILESTONES IN SPACE EXPLORATION

Since the mid-1950s, space has been explored by many types of spacecraft. Satellites, rockets, probes (to the Moon and between the planets) and shuttles have supplied us with a wealth of knowledge about our solar system.

4 October 1957	15 September 1959	12 April 1961	14 December 1962	31 July 1964	14 July 1965	1 March 1966
Sputnik 1 (USSR) First satellite launched into space.	*Luna 2* (USSR) First rocket reached the Moon.	*Vostok 1* (USSR) Yuri Gagarin first human in space.	*Mariner 2* (USA) Flew past Venus.	*Ranger 7* (USA) Close-range photographs of Moon.	*Mariner 4* (USA) Flew past Mars.	*Venera 3* (USSR) Landed on Venus

PLANET FACTS

A comparison of the planets that make up our solar system shows the vast differences between them.

PLANET	DISTANCE FROM SUN (million km/miles)	MASS (as a fraction of Earth's mass)	DIAMETER (as a fraction of Earth's diameter)	NUMBER OF MOONS
Mercury	58 (36)	0.06	0.4	0
Venus	108 (67)	0.8	0.9	0
Earth	150 (93)	1.0	1.0	1
Mars	228 (141)	0.1	0.5	2
Jupiter	778 (482)	318	11.2	16
Saturn	1,427 (885)	95	9.4	18
Uranus	2,871 (1,780)	14.5	4.0	15
Neptune	4,497 (2,788)	17	3.9	8
Pluto	5,913 (3,666)	0.002	0.2	1

METEOR SHOWERS

These are caused by the debris left by comets. The main annual meteor showers and their dates (which can vary by one day) are shown below. The number of meteors you see depends on the strength of the shower (sometimes as many as 50 meteors in one hour), how much moonlight is in the sky and whether you are watching them from a city or country area.

NAME OF SHOWER	DATE OF MAXIMUM ACTIVITY	COMMENT
Quadrantids	3 January	last only a few hours
Lyrids	22 April	from Comet Thatcher—produce some very bright meteors
Eta Aquarids	5 May	from Comet Halley
Delta Aquarids	30 July	a strong shower, especially with the help of the Perseids
Perseids	12 August	from Comet Swift-Tuttle
Orionids	22 October	from Comet Halley
Taurids	3–5 November	from Comet Encke—fireballs
Leonids	18 November	from Comet Tempel-Tuttle—major storm possible in 1999
Geminids	14 December	these and Perseids are the year's best showers

20 July 1969	3 December 1973	20 July 1976	1 September 1979	24 January 1986	6 March 1986	25 August 1989
Apollo 11 (USA) Humans landed on the Moon.	*Pioneer 10* (USA) Flew past Jupiter.	*Viking 1* (USA) Landed on Mars to search for life.	*Pioneer 11* (USA) Flew past Saturn.	*Voyager 2* (USA) Flew past Uranus.	*Vega 1* (USSR) Photographs of Comet Halley.	*Voyager 2* (USA) Flew past Neptune.

Index

Picture Credits

(t=top, b=bottom, l=left, r=right, c=centre, F=front, C=cover, B=back, Bg=background)
Ad-Libitum, 8l (S. Bowey). **Anglo-Australian Observatory**, 43br, 43cr, 47r (D. Malin). **AKG, Berlin**, 6tr (The Louvre); 3, 8br, 9cl. **AT & T Archives**, 11br. **Austral International**, 20bl (Camera Press), 33tr (Fotos International), 5br, 51cr (FPG), 22cl, 25tr (Rex Features), 14c (Rex Features/NASA), 11tl (Sipa Press/F. Zullo). **Australian Picture Library**, 37br (J. Blair), 4bl (E.T. Archive/Royal Society), 17bl (Orion Press), 51br (UPPA), 6bl (West Stock), 42bl. **Leo Enright**, 39tr. **Akira Fujii**, 17br, 20t. **Giraudon**, 30c (Lauros). **The Granger Collection**, 6tl, 7tc, 7tl, 7tr, 9br, 23br, 29bc, 29br, 31bc, 34tr, 35c, 53tc, 53tr. **Franz X. Kohlhauf**, 20/21. **David Levy**, 38tr (Sky Publishing Corporation). 33br. **Mt Stromlo and Siding Spring Observatories, A.N.U.**, 49bl. **NASA**, 46br. **Newell Colour**, 22bl. **The Photo Library, Sydney**, 19br (B. Belknap), 18b (A. Husmo), 37bl (R. Smith), 23tr, 35bc (SPL), 14bl (SPL/J. Baum), 44bl, 45br (SPL/C. Butler), 15br (SPL/J. Finch), 35br (SPL/G.

Garradd), 46/47t (SPL/T. Hallas), 35tl, 52bl (SPL/D. Hardy), 55cl (SPL/D. Milon), 17tr, 24tl, 27cr, 30bl, 37cr (SPL/NASA), 40/41c (SPL/G. Post), 14tr, 40cl (SPL/R. Royer). **Planet Earth Pictures**, 20c, 20cl (R. Chesher). **Stock Photos**, 20cr (J.P. Endress), 14br (Phototake). **Tom Stack & Associates**, 25cr (NASA), 28bc, 28bl (NASA/JPL), 25tc (USGS).

Illustration Credits

Gregory Bridges, 50tr, 50b/51c, 52/53c, 54br. **Lynette R. Cook**, 5tr, 8/9t, 10tr, 11b, 10/11c, 12/13c, 34/35c, 55c, 55cr. **Christer Eriksson**, 16/17c, 22/23c. **Robert Hynes**, 28/29c, 42/43c. **Mike Lamble**, 41tr, 43tr, 47bc, 48cl, 49br, 48/49t, 54tl, 54cl. **James McKinnon**, 38bl, 38/39c. **Peter Mennim**, 1, 26/27c. **Darren Pattenden/Garden Studio**, 32tr, 32/33c, 33tr, 41bl. **Oliver Rennert**, 2, 4ci, 12i, 14i, 16i, 17i, 18cl, 18cr, 18/19c, 18i, 20i, 22i, 24c, 26i, 28i, 29i, 30i, 32i, 36i, 37i, 38i, 40i, 41i, 43i, 51i. **Trevor Ruth**, 24/25c, 30/31c, 31tr. **Ray Sim**, 20tcr, 21tr. **Kevin

Stead**, 4tl, 36/37c, 37c, 55br. **Steve Trevaskis**, 6/7c, 44/45c, 44cl, 55tr. **Rod Westblade**, 4ti, 5i, 6i, 8i, 9i, 10i, 11i, 34i, 42i, 44i, 45i, 46i, 47i, 48i, 49i, 50i, 52i, endpapers. **Simon Williams/Garden Studio**, 4/5c, 14/15c.

Cover Credits

Anglo-Australian Observatory, FCcl (D. Malin). **Gregory Bridges**, BCtl. **Lynette R. Cook**, Bg, FCtr, FCtl. **The Photo Library, Sydney**, FCc (SPL/NASA). **Oliver Rennert**, BCtr. **Kevin Stead**, BCbr.